MW00489305

present it

present it

New Ideas for Stylish Garnishes

RUNNING PRESS
PHILADELPHIA · LONDON

A QUINTET BOOK

© 1999 by Quintet Publishing Limited

First published in the United States of America in 1999
by Running Press Book Publishers

All rights reserved under the Pan-American and International
Copyright Conventions.

Printed in China by Leefung-Asco Printers Ltd.

This book may not be reproduced in whole or in part, in any form
or by any means, electronic or mechanical, including photocopying,
recording, or by any information storage or retrieval system now
known or hereafter invented, without written permission from the
Publisher and copyright holder.

9 8 7 6 5 4 3 2 1

Digit on the right indicates the number of this printing

ISBN 0-7624-0502-3

Library of Congress
Cataloging-in-Publication Number 98-67644

This book was designed and produced by
Quintet Publishing Limited
6 Blundell Street
London N7 9BH

Creative Director: Rebecca Martin
Design: Deep Creative, London
Project Editor: Debbie Foy
Editor: Deborah Gray

Typeset in Great Britain by
Central Southern Typesetters, Eastbourne

This book may be ordered by mail from the publisher.
Please include $2.50 for postage and handling.
But try your bookstore first!

Running Press Book Publishers
125 South Twenty-second Street
Philadelphia, Pennsylvania 19103-4399

Material in this book has previously appeared in Quintet titles.

> **Because of the slight risk of salmonella, raw
> eggs should not be served to the very young,
> the ill or the elderly, or to pregnant women.**

contents

introduction

It's the little touches that make the meal, and no matter how good the food tastes, the initial impression rests on how good the food looks. A garnish is an affectionate gesture designed to impress your guests as well as complement the food.

With people becoming more interested in all aspects of food and its preparation, there seems no end to the range and ingenuity of garnishes. Some are based on traditional American cooking, but besides them has grown up a whole new concept of garnishing: a renaissance inspired by ideas and ingredients from a vast range of culinary cultures—Japanese to Mexican, from the Americas to the Middle East, Europe to the Pacific Rim—each with a tradition of respect, for both the food and its recipient.

Some garnishes do take a good deal of forethought and some skill and practice to perfect, but armed with **present it**'s clearly written text and excellent illustrations you will soon be a master of the art of garnishing. The effort is rewarded when you present your salad in the iced bowl that you have so artfully prepared; so simple yet so effective. Guests don't have to be concerned with squirting lemon juice and flying pits when you bring on your lemon in a wrap. For those less ambitious days there are plenty of simple ideas that take just seconds to make. A simple chile flower, a lemon fan or perhaps some frosted cranberries can transform an everyday meal into a special dish.

It is said that a dish should be a feast for the eyes as well as the stomach. Never underestimate the power of the senses as the meal is brought to the table. Time spent on intricate preparation is rewarded by the sight, the smell, the taste and, probably, the round of applause!

present it will show you, step-by-step, how to turn any meal into a celebration, and any dish into a work of art.

equipment and utensils

While many labor-saving utensils are available to assist in the art of garnishing, the main tools of the trade are a good work surface or chopping board, a sharp paring knife and a pair of scissors. These will see you through many of the step-by-step procedures in **present it**.

However, as your enthusiasm and confidence in making these garnishes grows, you might want to try some of the specialized equipment available. Some of the most useful are pictured below.

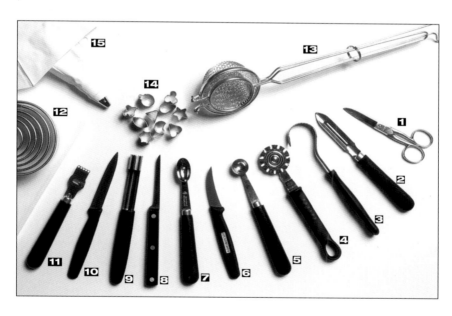

1	SCISSORS	9	CORER
2	VEGETABLE PEELER	10	PARING KNIFE
3	BUTTER CURLER	11	GROOVED CITRUS STRIPPER
4	FLUTED PASTRY CUTTER	12	PLAIN PASTRY CUTTERS
5	SMALL MELON BALLER	13	SMALL HINGED FRYING BASKET
6	CURVED TOOLING KNIFE	14	FANCY CUTTERS
7	OVAL FRUIT/VEGETABLE BALLER	15	PIPING BAG AND TUBE
8	TOOLING KNIFE		

how to choose a garnish

present it will show you something of the range of possible garnishes, with serving suggestions and variations on the most popular themes.

Some garnishes arise from time-honored combinations, like lemons with fish, apples with pork, sage and onions with goose, and cranberries with turkey, while others stem naturally from one of the dish's components: Tarragon Chicken, for example, simply crowned with a sprig of that aromatic herb.

Still other garnishes are chosen specifically for contrast, whether in color, texture, richness, or flavor: pink shrimp against the delicate green of an avocado mousse; crisp croûtons in a creamy soup; fresh salad vegetables with a smooth pâté; a slice of seasoned butter to moisten broiled fish; the sharp simplicity of a twist of lime on a venison terrine; chilled cucumber cooling a spicy curry.

Remember that a garnish is there to enhance the food, not to disguise it, and your choice of serving dish contributes to this. Elaborate patterns can distract the eye while plain colors and simple, elegant shapes will enhance your work of art and set it off to its best advantage.

So, with **present it**, a steady hand, and a vast array of possible ingredients to inspire you, you should be able to find the perfect garnish for any dish—and even invent a few of your own.

garnish it

fruit

apple peony

Use as a garnish for:

PÂTÉS AND TERRINES

HOT AND COLD PORK DISHES

VEGETABLE AND SALAD DISHES

1 Have ready a bowl of well salted water with a little lemon juice added.

Cut a dessert apple in half lengthwise. Lay it cut side down. With a sharp knife, cut apple from stalk to stem in paper-thin slices.

2 Drop slices into prepared bowl of water. Leave for half an hour. The salt will make the apple more pliable, and lemon juice will prevent discoloration.

3 Take one small apple slice and roll it up to form the center bud. Place apple bud skin side down.

4 Arrange remaining apple slices, skin side down and overlapping slightly, around bud.

5 Use a spatula to turn apple garnish the right way up and lift into position.

frosted cranberries

Use as a garnish for:

TERRINES AND PÂTÉS

COLD MEAT PLATTERS

ROAST TURKEY AND GAME BIRD DISHES

CHEESEBOARDS

1 Select ripe cranberries, or other red berries, and separate into small bunches. Brush with beaten egg white (see note, page 4).

2 Lightly sprinkle fruit with a coating of superfine sugar.

3 Form into small clusters and leave on a wire rack to dry thoroughly.

4 Arrange clusters, tucking a couple of small mint leaves in between them.

Variation The same method can be applied to black and green grapes, and, if decorating a dessert, dredge heavily with sugar.

melon grapes

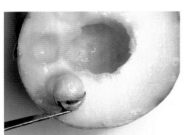

Use as a garnish for:

CHEESEBOARDS

HORS D'OEUVRES

TERRINES AND PÂTÉS

SALADS

COLD FISH, MEAT, AND POULTRY DISHES

1 Any variety of ripe melon can be used to make this miniature bunch of grapes. Cut melon in half, scoop out seeds and discard.

2 Using smallest melon baller, scoop out six balls for each garnish.

3 Arrange the balls on the serving plate, in a triangular shape, with two cilantro or flat parsley leaves at the top to represent vine leaves, and a piece of chive stem for the stalk.

4 More melon balls can be built up to form a larger bunch of grapes, say, 20 or 30, to garnish meat, fish, and cheese platters.

carambola flowers

Use as a garnish for:

TERRINES AND PÂTÉS

CHICKEN AND PORK DISHES

COLD MEATS

1 The unique shape of this fruit makes it a natural garnish.

Select a fruit which does not have too many blemishes. If necessary, finely pare down points of star to remove discolored or rough skin.

2 Slice carambola to approximately ¼-inch thick slices.

3 Use sliced carambola on its own, or with another fruit such as kiwi, or form into a flower using chive stems and herb leaves to make up design.

pineapple nut slices

Use as a garnish for:

PORK, HAM, AND
CHICKEN DISHES

1 Select a small, ripe but firm pineapple. Cut it into ¾-inch slices. Using a small plain cutter, remove core of pineapple.

2 Select a larger cutter to remove coarse outer skin of fruit.

3 Lightly flour pineapple slices, and then dip in beaten egg.

4 Coat thoroughly with almond flakes or shredded coconut.

5 Shallow fry in butter or oil, until a golden color. Drain on paper towel. Serve plain, or fill center hole with strawberry or maraschino cherry slices, or a fresh herb sprig.

poached pears

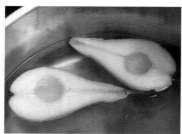

Use as a garnish for:

PORK, DUCK, GOOSE, AND GAME
(PARTICULARLY ROAST) DISHES

POACHED FISH DISHES

CHEESE DISHES

1 Select small, firm, but ripe pears. Peel the fruit. Have ready a bowl of water with a little lemon juice added to prevent discoloration.

Cut each pear in half lengthwise and then, with a melon baller, scoop out core to form a small cavity.

Cut a fine slice off base of pear so it will sit upright.

2 Prepare a light sugar syrup by dissolving ½ cup sugar in 1¼ cups water and 1 tablespoon lemon juice over a low heat, then boiling for about 2 to 3 minutes. Add pears and gently simmer until slightly softened (10 to 15 minutes, depending upon ripeness of fruit.)

Drain fruit on paper towel and keep warm or allow to cool before serving.

3 Fill cavity with mixture of chopped nuts and dried fruit.

Use as a garnish for:

SOUPS

SALADS

MEAT, POULTRY, AND GAME DISHES

CURRIES AND ASIAN DISHES

FLANS

1 Using a vegetable peeler or sharp paring knife, cut peel thinly from fruit.

2 Using point of knife, scrape away any bitter white pith.

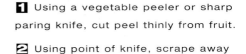

3 Trim strips of rind into neat lengths and then carefully cut into delicate, matchstick-wide strips.

4 Blanch in boiling water for 2 to 3 minutes, refresh in cold water, then pat dry on paper towels.

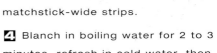

Variation Julienne strips can also be made from grapefruit, lemons, limes, or any other firm-skinned citrus fruit.

lime basket

Use as a garnish for:

COLD MEAT

SHELLFISH AND FISH PLATTERS

INDIVIDUAL MOUSSES AND TERRINES

BAKED WHOLE FISH DISHES

1 Select a good lime and take a fine sliver off the side so it will sit securely. Make two cuts halfway through the lime, ¼ inch apart, just either side of center; this will form the handle.

2 Slice across middle to meet first horizontal cuts. Remove the wedge of lime. Repeat on other side. Carefully cut away semi-circle of flesh from under handle and scoop out all the flesh in base of basket.

3 Fill the miniature basket with tiny sprigs of herbs or edible greenery, such as Scallion Brushes (page 28) or Chile Flowers (page 26).

Variation The basket can also be made from lemons and oranges, but these look better on larger serving platters.

lemon in a wrap

Use as a garnish for:

FISH AND SHELLFISH DISHES AND IN
DISHES WHERE FRESHLY SQUEEZED
JUICE IS REQUIRED

1 Cut out a round of cheesecloth,
measuring 8 inches across.

2 Cut small lemon or lime in half
and place one half in center of
cheesecloth, cut side down. Draw up
edges to form a small pouch.

3 Tie up neck of lemon wrap with
thread, trimming away loose ends.

4 Using fresh herbs as available,
tuck small sprigs around neck
of lemon wrap.

twisted lemon fans

Use as a garnish for:

HORS D'OEUVRES

PÂTÉS AND MOUSSES

FISH AND SHELLFISH

ROAST CHICKEN AND VEAL DISHES

1 Using a sharp paring knife or special citrus grooving knife, make grooves along length of lemons from end to end.

2 Cut into slices ¼ inch thick, but finer if they are to be twisted. Cut three slices for each garnish needed.

Lay cut slices one on top of the other, and twist the two outer surfaces into opposite directions.

3 Separate the twists slightly to form a fan. You can place onto a whole lemon slice, to serve.

iced citrus bowl

Use as a garnish for:

SHELLFISH

SORBETS AND WATER ICES

1 Have ready two glass freezerproof bowls, one slightly larger than the other, and room in the freezer to accommodate them.

Fill the larger of the two bowls with 1 inch water (*boiled* water will give clearer ice). Add some fruit slices, herbs, etc, and freeze until solid.

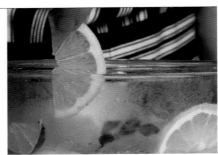

2 Place second bowl inside large bowl. Position it centrally and weight it down (use packs of frozen food to do this). Pour 1 inch water between the two bowls, add some more garnishes and freeze again.

3 To release smaller bowl, remove weights, rub inside of bowl with a hot, damp cloth or fill with warm water. Carefully loosen and remove.

4 To remove outer bowl, fill sink with warm water and sit bowl to just below its rim in water until it loosens. Do not allow the iced bowl to begin melting.

Store in freezer in a large plastic bag or use immediately.

kiwi fans

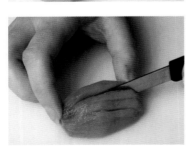

Use as a garnish for:

SALADS, PÂTÉS, AND MOUSSES

FISH, CHICKEN, AND GAME DISHES

COLD MEAT PLATTERS

1 Select firm, small kiwi fruits and peel, using a sharp paring knife.

2 Cut the kiwi in half, lengthwise, and then again into quarters.

3 Cut five or six slices along length of kiwi as shown, stopping just short of the end.

4 With the point of a knife, carefully ease slices open, and fan them out.

5 A small decorative chive "bow," a fresh herb sprig, or a small slice of strawberry can add a final touch.

adorn it

vegetable

chile flowers

Use as a garnish for:

TERRINES, PÂTÉS, AND MOUSSES

HOT, SPICY DISHES (MEXICAN AND THAI IN PARTICULAR)

1 The stalk ends of small red or green chile peppers are used for this garnish. Cut to desired length. Slide a small paring knife around inside of chile to loosen core and seeds, and remove them.

2 Using scissors, cut around length of chile to form petals, trimming tips of each petal to a point.

3 Drop the chile flowers into iced water and leave for 1 to 1½ hours to allow them to "blossom."

Use as a garnish for:

MOUSSES, PÂTÉS, AND TERRINES
ALMOST ANY COLD MEAT
FISH OR VEGETABLE DISHES
EGG DISHES

1 Select medium-sized, firm, ripe tomatoes. With a small, sharp paring knife and starting at non-stalk end of tomato, slice a continuous paper-thin strip of skin ½ inch wide, and cut in a circular fashion around the tomato to produce a spiral.

2 Using stem end of the strip to form center of rose, carefully wind tomato peel around itself, skin side out.

3 When completely wound, shape skin into a rose, making "petals" more open around base of flower. A couple of bay or mint leaves add a final touch.

scallion brushes and bows

Use as a garnish for:

CHINESE COOKERY

MEAT DISHES

DIPS

FLANS

EGG AND RICE DISHES

SALADS

1 To make **Scallion Brushes**, select medium-sized scallions. Trim off roots and remove any coarse outer leaves. Cut scallion to approximately 4 inches in length.

With a sharp knife, make a cut down its length to within 1½ inches of the root end. Rotate a quarter turn and make another cut down stem.

Continue making as many fine cuts down stem as possible, to form thin strands. Repeat this process with remaining scallions.

2 Drop the scallions into cold water, and refrigerate. Within the hour they will have curled.

3 For **Scallion Bows**, select medium-sized scallions and remove any coarse outer leaves. Trim root and first ½ inch of bulb end. Cut scallion to approximately 4 inches in length.

To form bows, make cuts from both ends of scallion to within 1 inch of the center. As with the Scallion Brush, rotate and continue making fine cuts to produce a "bow-tie" effect.

carrot and cucumber curls

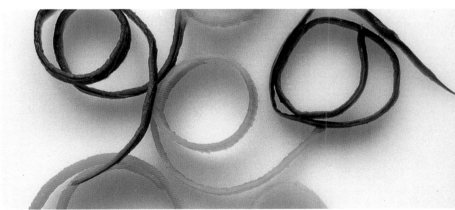

Use as a garnish for:

SOUPS

SALADS

HORS D'OEUVRES AND MEAT PLATTERS

FISH AND MOUSSES

1 Select young vegetables—bright in color and a good straight shape. With a vegetable peeler, peel away fine, even strips. For cucumber curls, only the dark green skin can be used. Carrot curls can be made from whole vegetable.

2 Roll up slices, secure with a toothpick and put in a bowl.

3 Alternatively, pack tightly into ice cube trays or plastic egg containers. Cover with cold water and then position bowl or trays in coldest part of refrigerator for 6 to 24 hours.

4 Drain away water, discard toothpicks and gently uncoil the rolls to form decorative curls.

cucumber fans
and fleurs-de-lys

MOUSSES AND PÂTÉS

COLD FISH AND SEAFOOD DISHES

COLD MEAT PLATTERS

VEGETABLE AND RICE SALADS

1 For a **Cucumber Fan**,
cut a 3-inch piece from a length
of cucumber. Cut this in half
lengthwise. Then make a lengthwise
cut along one of the halves deep
enough to remove seeds.

2 Using a sharp paring knife
or grooving tool, cut out V-shaped
grooves along length of outside
of cucumber.

3 Lay cucumber on its flat
base and, with a sharp knife,
diagonally cut a corner off one
end. Use remaining pointed
corner as tip of fan.

4 Cut five to ten paper-thin slices to tip of cucumber, taking care not to cut right through tip. On final slice cut right through to separate fan from remaining cucumber. Gently press cucumber slices so that they "fan" out.

5 A **Cucumber Fleur-de-Lys** is made by following the steps above to make a seven-slice fan. Then, bend second, fourth and sixth slice toward joined end of fan, forming small plumes. Arrange Fleur-de-Lys, fold side down.

onion chrysanthemum

Use as a garnish for:

TERRINES AND PÂTÉS

COLD MEATS

FLANS

PIES

SALADS

1 Select a small, firm, white or red onion. Peel away the fine paper skin. Trim away stem and root.

Sit onion firmly on its base and, with a small, sharp knife, make a series of criss-cross incisions, at approximately ¼-inch intervals. Do not cut right through to base.

2 Let some onion pieces fall away. Gently tease apart the onion to form a tight chrysanthemum flower.

3 Arrange singly, or in a group with a couple of bay leaves.

Variation The edge of the onion can be "blushed" pink with a little food coloring. Shallots and pickling onions can also be used to make miniature chrysanthemums.

radish bud and marguerite

Use as a garnish for:

PÂTÉS AND TERRINES

SALADS AND COLD MEAT PLATTERS

1 To make a **Radish Bud**, select a round, unblemished radish. Wash and cut a fine slice off stalk end. Turn radish over. Using a sharp paring knife, make four vertical and six horizontal cuts, stopping short of base of radish—do not slice right through it.

2 Drop radish "bud" into iced water, where it will take from 30 minutes to an hour to begin to open.

3 To make a **Radish Marguerite**, initially prepare radish as for a bud, then, using a small sharp paring knife, cut four to six leaf-shapes, into red skin only, from top center almost down to stalk end. Ease the red "petals" away with knife point, leaving lower ends attached.

4 Drop radish into iced water, where it will take from 30 minutes to an hour to begin to open.

bell pepper cut-outs

Use as a garnish for:

HORS D'OEUVRES AND CANAPÉS

ASPIC DISHES

TERRINES, PÂTÉS, AND MOUSSES

EGG DISHES

COLD MEAT DISHES

1 The bright, shiny skins of bell peppers are ideal for making decorative shapes, and add instant color to many dishes.

To prepare peppers, wipe and then cut off a fairly thick slice at stalk end.

2 Remove white pith and seeds with a knife. Now the pepper can be sliced either across, or lengthwise, and cut into desired shapes.

vegetable coils

Use as a garnish for:

BORDERING MEAT AND FISH PLATTERS

DECORATIVE SALADS

1 Select small, tender vegetables which are straight in shape. Carrots, cucumbers, zucchini, and daikon are all suitable for this garnish. If using carrots or zucchini, boil first until *al dente* and then refresh in iced water, to make them a little more tender and pliable to work with.

2 Trim to 3 to 4 inches in length. Insert either a wooden skewer or chopstick through center of vegetable from end to end.

3 With a small, sharp knife, starting ¼ inch from end of vegetable, slice through to the wooden skewer. Firmly holding knife at a slight angle, turn vegetable and continue cutting around wooden skewer, in a spiral action.

4 Remove skewer and gently tease apart the vegetable to form a decorative coil.

Variation The center of the cucumber or zucchini can be easily scooped out to produce a more delicate-looking coil.

potato baskets
and nests

FOWL AND GAME DISHES

BROILED OR POACHED FISH

1 For **Potato Baskets**, peel
and very thinly slice some firm,
waxy potatoes. For **Potato Nests**,
shred the potatoes or cut into
fine straws. Soak potato in cold
water for 30 minutes. Drain and
dry thoroughly.

2 Dip a hinged frying
basket into some hot oil
to prevent potatoes from
sticking. Remove and
line frying basket with
either overlapping slices
of potato or the shredded
or straw potatoes.

Deep fry potato basket or
nest in hot oil (350°F)
until a light golden color.
Remove and drain frying
basket. Allow to cool
slightly before carefully
removing cooked potato.

3 Make up quantity of baskets or nests required and then either reheat in a hot oven, 400°F, or by carefully refrying as above until a dark golden color.

4 Serve immediately, filled with baby mushrooms, onions, glazed or puréed vegetables, or Bacon Rolls (page 50).

parisian potato balls

Use as a garnish for:

MEAT, GAME, CHICKEN, AND FISH DISHES—PARTICULARLY BROILED AND ROAST CUTS

ALSO AS A VEGETABLE ACCOMPANIMENT

1 Sieve some cooked mashed potato. Beat in one egg yolk for each 1 pound potatoes. Season with salt, pepper, and a little freshly grated nutmeg.

2 Take a spoonful of potato mixture and roll it between lightly floured hands to form a smooth round ball the size of a cherry. To ensure even-sized potato balls, it is a good idea to measure or weigh each spoonful.

3 Dip each potato ball in beaten egg. Using two forks coat potato balls in fine, dry bread crumbs. Alternatively, after coating with the egg, roll potato balls in slivered almonds or chopped hazelnuts until well coated.

4 Deep-fat fry (350°F) until golden brown. Drain on paper towels. Keep warm until required.

potato allumettes

Use as a garnish for:

HOT GAME AND MEAT DISHES

BROILED MEAT AND FISH DISHES

1 *Allumettes* is the French word for "matches," a perfect description of this potato garnish.

Peel and thinly slice (approximately 1/8 inch) some firm, waxy potatoes. Trim stacked slices into an even oblong or square, 1 1/2 inches in length. Slice through potatoes at 1/8-inch intervals to produce matchsticks.

Soak in cold water for at least 30 minutes. Drain and dry thoroughly.

2 Deep fry in hot oil (375°F) for just a few minutes or until a dark golden color.

3 Drain on paper towels, sprinkle with salt, and serve immediately.

zucchini boats

Use as a garnish for:

HOT AND COLD MEAT

VEGETABLE DISHES

EGG AND FISH DISHES

1 Select large-sized, green zucchini. Split each in half lengthwise, cut into 3-inch lengths. Using a small paring knife, carve ends to form a boat shape.

2 Take a fine slice off underside to give "boat" a secure base to sit on. With a teaspoon or grapefruit knife, hollow out zucchini boat to within 1/4 inch of edge. Prepare remaining wedges of zucchini in same way.

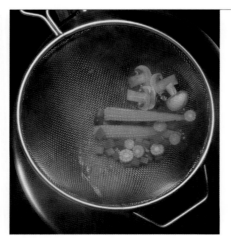

3 Prepare some tiny colorful vegetables—carrots, baby corn slices, baby mushroom slices, peas, or broccoli flowerets.

Blanch zucchini boats and vegetables in boiling, salted water until *al dente*. Drain and toss in butter if to be served hot.

4 Fill zucchini boats with a cargo of vegetables and topped with tiny, fresh herb sprigs.

julienne bundles

1 Choose a colorful assortment of vegetables, such as zucchini, carrot, celery, green beans, and swede. Trim, peel, and cut into thin strips—*à la julienne*—approximately 2½ inches x ¼ inch.

2 Blanch vegetables julienne in boiling water for 1 minute. Drain and glaze with a little butter if to be served hot; alternatively, refresh in iced water, and drain.

3 Form assorted vegetables julienne into small bundles and secure together with an onion ring or a fine chive stem tied in a knot.

turned mushroom caps

Use as a garnish for:

(SAUTÉED FOR) ALL MEAT
AND POULTRY DISHES

EGG, RICE, AND PASTA DISHES

(RAW WITH) PÂTÉS, SALADS, COLD
MEATS, OR POULTRY DISHES

1 Select fresh, white, medium-sized button mushrooms. Wipe them clean with a damp cloth.

Hold mushroom stem in one hand, and the blade of a sharp paring knife between first finger and thumb of the other hand. Repeatedly draw knife down center to the base of mushroom cap in a curved, sickle fashion. On each groove ensure that each alternate cut is at a flatter angle so that the piece of mushroom will come cleanly away.

2 Trim stalk and drop each mushroom into a bowl of water with a little lemon juice added to prevent discoloration while you prepare the rest.

3 The drained mushrooms can either be sautéed in butter, or used raw as a garnish for salads and pâtés.

dill pickle fans

Use as a garnish for:

PÂTÉS, TERRINES, AND MOUSSES

EGG AND MEAT DISHES

1 Drain dill pickles well. Make five parallel incisions through length of dill pickle but do not cut right down to end.

2 Press slices apart with flat side of a knife blade to form a fan. Lay a fine strip of red, canned pimento around neck of dill pickle fan, to form a decorative band.

green laces

Use as a garnish for:

SOUPS

EGG AND VEGETABLE DISHES

BROILED MEAT AND FISH

CASSEROLES AND SAUCES

1 Select tender young leeks. Trim away any coarse outer leaves and wash thoroughly. Cut white part of leek away and use for soups or as a vegetable.

2 With a sharp, pointed knife, halve leek lengthwise. Then separate the layers and cut them lengthwise into "laces" about ¼-inch wide.

3 Blanch "laces" in a pan of boiling salted water for 30 to 40 seconds. Drain and glaze with a knob of butter.

accompany i

meat & fish

miniature kabobs

Use as a garnish for:

EGG AND CHEESE DISHES

ROAST AND BROILED MEATS

POULTRY

FISH

CRÊPES AND OMELETS

RICE AND PASTA DISHES

OR SERVE AS AN APPETIZER

1 Select a variety of small and colorful food such as Bacon Rolls (page 50), baby corn (sliced), button mushrooms, shrimp, red and yellow bell peppers, cherry tomatoes, cubes of ham, pineapple, apricots, and thin slices of fresh ginger.

Cook vegetables until *al dente*. Refresh in cold water and drain thoroughly. Cut selected fruits, meats, and vegetables into roughly even-sized pieces.

2 Thread onto wooden toothpicks or short wooden skewers (maximum 4 inches in length).

Brush liberally with melted butter or oil and cook under a preheated broiler, turning frequently, until cooked. Cooking time will vary according to types of food used.

3 Serve immediately, topped with fresh sprigs of herbs.

Note Select foods that will most enhance and complement your chosen main dish, such as pineapple, bell peppers, and fresh ginger for pork and ham dishes, or bacon rolls, mushrooms, and tomatoes for broiled poultry, fish, and meat dishes.

bacon rolls

Use as a garnish for:

ROAST CHICKEN OR TURKEY

SMOKED HADDOCK DISHES

OMELETS AND OTHER EGG DISHES

OR TOSSED IN GREEN SALAD

1 Select some sliced bacon. Remove any rind and bones with a pair of scissors.

Cut each slice into two or three pieces. With the blade of a sharp knife, held at an angle, stretch bacon using firm stroking movements.

2 Roll up each bacon slice and secure with a wooden toothpick. Cook bacon rolls under a hot broiler, turning frequently to ensure an even color and crispness. Alternatively, bake in a preheated oven at 400°F.

asparagus tips
with parma ham

Use as a garnish for:

MOUSSES, PÂTÉS, AND VEGETABLE
TERRINES

EGG DISHES

COLD MEAT AND FISH PLATTERS

OR ON TOASTS AS INDIVIDUAL CANAPÉS

1 Select tender young asparagus tips. Cut into 2-inch lengths. Cook until *al dente*. Drain and refresh in iced water. Drain thoroughly.

2 Cut Parma ham into strips long enough to wrap around one or two asparagus tips twice, and cover two-thirds of the length of asparagus, revealing just the tip.

3 Lay asparagus rolls on their seam and lightly glaze with aspic jelly.

4 Garnish each roll with a bow made from a small strand of fresh chive or canned pimento, or with tiny hard-cooked egg shapes and red or black caviar or lumpfish roe.

smoked salmon cornets

Use as a garnish for:

FISH DISHES

SEAFOOD, AVOCADO, OR CUCUMBER

HORS D'OEUVRES AND PÂTÉS

MOUSSES

EGG DISHES

1 Cut some thin slices of smoked salmon into circles, using a 3½-inch diameter pastry cutter. Cut each circle into quarters.

2 Roll each quarter into a conical shape. Position three cornets on the plate and pipe a little cream cheese or savory butter into their centers.

3 Top piped cream with a little lumpfish roe or caviar, and tuck a sprig of fresh dill, fennel, or another delicate herb around base of cornets.

crunchy bacon bits

Use as a garnish for:

SOUPS

EGG, SMOKED HADDOCK,
AND POTATO DISHES

MORNAY DISHES

GREEN, AVOCADO,
AND CAULIFLOWER SALADS

1 Select good sliced bacon. Using a pair of scissors, cut away any rind and bones. Snip bacon into small pieces.

2 Fry in its own fat in a non-stick pan, stirring frequently to ensure even cooking and color. When bacon bits are crunchy, drain on paper towels before using.

display it

bread & pastry

choux pastry swans

Use as a garnish for:

SAVORY MOUSSES AND MOLDS

FISH DISHES

OR AS CANAPÉS

1 Make up a quantity of choux paste (see opposite page). Fit a small piping bag with a plain tube. Spoon in one-third of the choux paste. Lightly grease a cookie sheet, and pipe out swans' heads and necks.

2 Using a star tube fitted in a second piping bag, use remaining choux paste to form the swans' bodies. Piping in a circular movement, form an oblong, which is slightly higher at one end. Repeat.

3 Glaze with beaten egg and sprinkle swan bodies with freshly grated Parmesan cheese. Cook at 400°F for 15 to 20 minutes, or until well risen and golden brown.

4 Cool "swans" before assembling. Split the bodies in half horizontally and then cut top half of body in half lengthwise to form two wings.

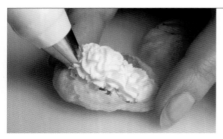

5 Pipe a savory butter, pâté, or cream cheese onto base of body. Secure neck and head in position and then replace wings.

unsweetened choux paste

Ingredients

MAKES APPROXIMATELY 8 OZ
1/2 CUP ALL-PURPOSE FLOUR
DASH OF SALT
4 TBSP (1/2 STICK) BUTTER
2/3 CUP WATER
2 EGGS, BEATEN

1 Sift flour and salt onto a piece of waxed paper. Put butter and water in a saucepan over a moderate heat and stir until butter has melted.

2 Bring mixture to a boil, switch off heat, and tip flour into pan all at once. Stir quickly with a wooden spoon until flour has absorbed all the liquid and forms into a clean ball. Beat in the eggs, a little at a time, until paste is shiny and thick enough to hold its own shape.

pastry garnishes for pies

Use as a garnish for:

SHELLFISH

SORBETS AND WATER ICES

1 A pastry-covered pie can be attractively garnished with pastry overs, to add an elegant touch to the dish.

For fish or chicken pies, special cutters are available to make pastry fish and chicken shapes. Otherwise, use a sharp knife and shape your own animals!

Refer to Pastry Fleurons (page 60) for some other ideas or shapes. These can then be brushed with an egg glaze and positioned on the pie. Bake pie according to your recipe.

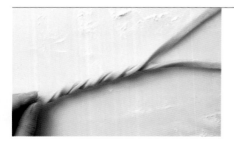

2 Braids and twists of pastry make a decorative border to a pie. For a twist, roll out two equal lengths of pastry, slightly longer than circumference of pie lid. Twist strips together and lay around edge of pie.

3 Pastry tassels make an ideal centerpiece. Cut a pastry strip 1 inch wide and about 6 inches long. Make cuts ¾ inch long at ¼-inch intervals, then roll up the strip. Place it on the pie and open out tassels.

pastry fleurons

Use as a garnish for:

CASSEROLES AND OTHER MEAT, FISH, AND GAME DISHES

1 A good stand-by in the freezer are sheets of puff pastry which can be simply transformed into decorative shapes by using small cutters and a sharp knife.

Using a plain cookie cutter, cut out crescents as shown. Heart shapes, letters, fish, and star shapes can also be made with special cutters.

2 Mark and cut out square shapes; cut in half diagonally to form triangles. Using the back of a knife or a skewer, mark out a criss-cross pattern. Cut out leaf shapes and mark veins with back of a knife or skewer.

3 Lay shapes on a damp cookie sheet, brush with an egg glaze, and bake in a preheated oven at 400°F for 7 to 10 minutes or until well risen, crisp, and golden brown.

pastry horns

Use as a garnish for:

MEAT, GAME, AND FISH DISHES

EGG AND CHEESE DISHES

1 Buy a good quality rough puff, flaky pastry, or phyllo pastry sheets. Thaw and refrigerate until required. Lightly grease the base end of some cream horn molds.

2 Thinly roll out pastry on a lightly floured board. Trim edges and cut into strips approximately ¼ inch wide.

Wind a strip of pastry round mold in an overlapping coil. Dampen loose end with a drop of water to secure it down.

3 Place horns on a buttered cookie sheet. Glaze with beaten egg and milk. Bake in a preheated oven at 325°F for 10 to 15 minutes or until golden brown and crisp.

4 Slip horns from their molds and cool on a wire rack. Fill with smooth pâté, cream cheese, or a vegetable purée, using a piping bag, and top with nuts, sliced olives, spices, or herbs.

poppadum baskets

HOT SPICY DISHES

CURRIES

SALADS

Poppadums are a wafer-thin East Indian bread made with lentil flour. They can be plain or seasoned with pepper, garlic, or a number of other flavorings.

1 Buy small, round poppadums—ideally, 4 to 5 inches in diameter. Heat some oil for deep frying. Holding a metal ladle in one hand and a spoon in the other, hold poppadum between the two utensils, and slowly lower into hot oil.

2 Fry for just a few seconds, until poppadum curls up around inner spoon, to form a shallow basket shape. When golden and crisp, remove from hot oil, drain thoroughly, and leave to cool on paper towel. Store in an airtight container until required.

3 Fill with finely diced tomatoes, cucumber, sweet bell peppers, or onions, and toasted, flaked, or shredded coconut before serving.

croûtons and croûtes

Use as a garnish for:

CREAM SOUPS

ALSO SPRINKLED OVER SALADS

1 Trim away crusts from several thick slices of whole wheat or white bread. (One-day-old bread is better than fresh.) Cut bread into ¼-inch cubes.

2 Heat an equal quantity of a good vegetable oil and unsalted butter. When the fat is foaming, toss in croûtons and stir continuously, ensuring cubes are evenly browned and cooked and crisp.

Drain croûtons on several layers of paper towel before serving.

3 Larger round, heart- or diamond-shaped croûtes can be cooked in the same way and used to garnish meat and chicken casseroles. Use pastry cutters to obtain desired shape.

Variation Frying in flavored butter, such as garlic, herb, or peppered butter can enhance the croûtons.

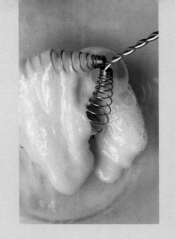

decorate it

butter & egg

butter curls

Use as a garnish for:

BROILED MEATS

VEGETABLES AND POTATOES

OR AS AN ATTRACTIVE WAY OF
PRESENTING BUTTER TO ACCOMPANY
BREAD, TOAST, OR CRACKERS

1 To obtain the perfect butter curl,
a butter curler is required. Dip it in hot
water before forming each curl.

Stand a chilled block of butter on its
side and firmly pull butter curler along
length of butter, from end to end,
to form the curl.

2 Drop curl into a bowl of iced water
until required.

coated butter rounds

Use as a garnish for:

BROILED STEAKS AND CHOPS

POTATOES BAKED IN THEIR SKINS

VEGETABLES

1 Coated butter rounds can be made by two different methods. The first is to use a melon baller which has been dipped in very hot water. Press cutter into firm butter and turn it firmly to produce a round. Drop the round into iced water until required.

2 Alternatively, cut a piece of butter approximately 1 inch square and roll it between two wet butter pats to obtain a round. Drop into icy water, as above.

3 The rounds can either be served plain, or rolled in finely chopped fresh herbs, paprika, crushed coriander seeds, mixed peppercorns, or finely chopped toasted hazelnuts.

4 If butter rounds are to be used as an accompaniment to bread or crackers, arrange them into a "bunch of grapes." Approximately 30 or 40 balls will be needed to make an impressive bunch. The stem and leaf can be cut out of butter, or cucumber skin.

specialty butters

Butters can also be flavored before forming into rounds, curls, or other shapes. Not only will it enrich and moisten the food but it will also coat it with a delicious buttery lemon or herb flavor. Here are a few ideas for flavoring butters before they are shaped or molded.

1 Caper Butter To 8 tablespoons (1 stick) butter, add 1 teaspoon crushed capers. Stir in ½ teaspoon each orange and lemon juice and ¼ cup drained, finely chopped anchovies. Shape into balls and chill. Use to accompany broiled fish.

2 Orange Butter To 8 tablespoons (1 stick) butter blend in 1 tablespoon each finely grated orange rind, orange juice, and green peppercorns. Spread ½-inch thick layer on foil and chill. Use to accompany fish, pork, chicken and game, and vegetables.

3 Red Bell Pepper Butter To 8 tablespoons (1 stick) butter beat in a pinch of ground ginger and a few drops of Tabasco sauce. Mix 3 tablespoons finely chopped red bell pepper. Form into a long roll. Wrap in foil and chill. Unwrap, coat in finely chopped parsley and slice. Use to accompany broiled meats, fish, baked potatoes, and vegetables.

4 Mustard Butter To 8 tablespoons (1 stick) butter beat in 1 tablespoon mustard, 6 drops Tabasco sauce and a dash of Worcestershire sauce. When light and fluffy, transfer to a piping bag with small plain tube and pipe three blobs close together onto foil. Repeat. Chill well. Decorate with tiny herb sprig. Use to accompany meats and fish.

5 Tomato Butter To 8 tablespoons (1 stick) butter beat in 2 teaspoons tomato paste. Chill, then form into balls. Use to accompany meat, fish, pasta, and vegetables.

6 Fresh Herb Butter To 8 tablespoons (1 stick) butter blend in 1 tablespoon freshly chopped mixed fresh herbs (chives, tarragon, and parsley). Form into a roll. Wrap in foil and chill. Slice the butter. Use to accompany meat, fish, and vegetables.

shredded crêpes

Use as a garnish for:

LIGHT SOUPS AND CONSOMMÉS

1 Make a batter using 1 cup
all-purpose flour, 3 eggs, ¼ cup
vegetable oil. Leave to stand
for 30 to 60 minutes, then add
2 tablespoons finely chopped
fresh herbs.

Cook a batch of thin crêpes. Allow
to cool, and stack between layers of
waxed paper.

2 Tightly roll up a couple of stacked
crêpes to form a cigar shape.

3 With a sharp knife, finely slice
rolled crêpe to form thin shreds.
Warm through in the oven before
sprinkling onto soups.

egg royale

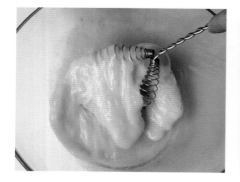 

Use as a garnish for:

CLEAR SOUPS AND CONSOMMÉS

1 Beat together 3 eggs and 1 cup hot stock. Season lightly with salt and fresh black pepper.

2 Sieve the custard through a fine mesh or piece of cheesecloth into a shallow cake pan, lined with waxed paper.

Stand the cake pan in a roasting pan containing 1/2 inch water and cook in a preheated oven at 300°F for about 40 minutes, or until firm to touch.

3 Cool, then carefully lift out the set custard using waxed paper lining as a cradle. Cut out fancy shapes using aspic and pastry cutters (dice, stars, moons, hearts).

chopped egg garni

Use as a garnish for:

DRESSED CRAB

FISH AND FLANS

MOUSSES

SALADS AND RICE DISHES

MAYONNAISE-BASED DISHES

1 Hard-cook one or two eggs, starting them off in cold water and allowing them 10 minutes' boiling time. Cool rapidly, then shell and separate yolk from white.

Pass yolk through a metal sieve, pressing with a wooden spoon.

2 Finely chop egg white and, either leave plain, or mix with finely chopped fresh parsley.

3 Use fine lines of alternating yolk and the speckled green egg whites.

4 The finely chopped parsley can be used as a third color, with the plain egg yolk and egg white, or the white can be dusted with paprika.

egg flowers

Use as a garnish for:

TERRINES, PÂTÉS, AND MOUSSES

COLD MEATS AND PIES

ASPIC-COATED DISHES

1 Hard-cook one or two eggs, then plunge into cold water immediately.

Using an egg slicer or stainless steel knife, slice or halve the egg according to garnish required.

2 The whites can then be cut into fancy shapes using small pastry cutters and piping tubes.

3 Sieved egg yolk can act as center of flower. Alternatively, cut out a round of yolk using a small, plain piping nozzle as a cutter.

4 Blanched cucumber peel can be used for bolder stem and leaf shapes. Chive stems and herb leaves will produce a more delicate garnish.

complete it

dessert

peanut brittle shards

Ingredients

MAKES 1 LB CARAMEL

1 LB RAW BROWN SUGAR

1/3 PT WATER

2 TBSP (1/4 STICK) BUTTER

2 TBSP CORN SYRUP

1 TSP VINEGAR

6 OZ NUTS, CHOPPED FINELY

1 Put ingredients into a heavy saucepan and stir over steady heat until sugar has dissolved. Bring to a boil and cook for 20 minutes. Add chopped nuts, and cook for a further 2 to 3 minutes before testing caramel by dropping a small amount into a cup of cold water: if caramel is brittle and cracks, then it is ready. Grease a sheet of waxed paper and place on a large cookie sheet.

2 Spread the caramel nut brittle thinly across waxed paper using a palette knife. Allow to set for 3 to 4 hours. Using a toffee hammer, break nut brittle into shards and serve with several scoops of ice cream.

caramel splashes

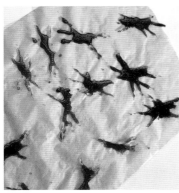

Ingredients

MAKES 1 LB CARAMEL

1 LB RAW BROWN SUGAR

$\frac{1}{3}$ PT WATER

2 TBSP ($\frac{1}{4}$ STICK) BUTTER

2 TBSP CORN SYRUP

1 TSP VINEGAR

1 Put ingredients into a heavy saucepan and stir over steady heat until sugar has dissolved. Bring to a boil and cook for approximately 20 to 25 minutes. Test caramel by dropping a small amount into a cup of cold water: if caramel is brittle and cracks, then it is ready for the next stage.

2 Grease a sheet of waxed paper and, using a teaspoon, scoop up some of the caramel and "splatter" it onto the waxed paper. Allow to set for 3 to 4 hours before serving.

chocolate curls

Ingredients

1 LB COOKING CHOCOLATE

VEGETABLE PEELER

1 Break chocolate into pieces and melt in a bowl over hot water. Spread thickly over a sheet of waxed paper and allow to set completely.

2 Using a vegetable peeler, gently take curls of the chocolate and use to serve with a whole range of desserts.

citrus swirls

Ingredients

2 LEMONS AND 2 LIMES

CITRUS STRIPPER

1 A citrus stripper is a special tool that cuts ¼-inch-wide strips from the rind of citrus fruits.

2 To create long strips (as shown), cut in a spiral shape around the fruit. To create short strips, pull the stripper from top to bottom of fruit.

almond tuilles

Ingredients

MAKES **25**

6 TBSP (**3/4** STICK) BUTTER

3/4 CUP SUPERFINE SUGAR

1/2 CUP ALL-PURPOSE FLOUR, SIFTED

1/2 CUP GROUND ALMONDS

1 Cream butter and sugar together. Stir in flour and almonds and mix thoroughly. Place teaspoonfuls of mixture well apart on a greased cookie sheet and flatten them with a damp fork. Bake at 400°F in a preheated oven for 6 to 8 minutes.

2 Remove from oven and allow to stand for 1 minute. Remove with a palette knife and mold warm biscuit around end of a rolling pin, forming the fluted shape with your fingers. Allow to cool completely before serving.

shortbread dessert cookies

Ingredients

MAKES 22

¹/₄ CUP SUPERFINE SUGAR

2 EGGS

VANILLA EXTRACT

¹/₂ CUP ALL-PURPOSE
FLOUR, SIFTED

SUPERFINE SUGAR,
FOR DREDGING

1 Whisk sugar, eggs, and vanilla together using an electric blender, then fold in the flour. Place mixture into a piping bag with a ¹/₂-inch plain tube and pipe into finger lengths on a cookie sheet. Dust well with superfine sugar and bake for 6 to 8 minutes at 375°F. Remove from oven and allow to cool for 5 minutes, then transfer to a wire rack for further cooling.

index